READING/WRITING CONNECTION

Thinking and Learning About Print

Parts A and B

PROGRAM AUTHORS

Marilyn Jager Adams
Carl Bereiter
Jan Hirshberg
Valerie Anderson

CONSULTING AUTHORS

Michael Pressley
Marsha Roit
Iva Carruthers
Bill Pinkney

OPEN COURT PUBLISHING COMPANY

Cover art by Nadine Bernard Westcott
Interior art by Nelle Davis, Susannah Ryan, and Jack Wallen
Composition, electronic page makeup and art management were provided by
Chestnut House Group, Inc.

Printed in the United States of America

ISBN 0-8126-1036-9

20 19 18 17 16 15 14 13 12 11

Name

Writing Letters

A

a

B

b

 Directions: Write as many letters as will fit on each line of these practice pages.

Letter Knowledge

Name

Lesson 2

Writing Letters

a b c d e f g h i j k l m n o p q r s t u v w x y z

A B C D E F G H I J K L M N O P Q R S T U V W X Y Z

C

c

D

d

E

e

Directions: Write as many letters as will fit on each line of these practice pages.

Name

A Writing Letters a b c d e f g h i j

B C D E F G H I J K L M N O

k l m n o p q r s t u v w x

P Q R S T U V W X Y Z z y

F

f

G

g

H

h

Directions: Write as many letters as will fit on each line of these practice pages.

Letter Knowledge

Name

Writing Letters

a b c d e f g h i j k l m n o p q r s t u v w x y z

A B C D E F G H I J K L M N O P Q R S T U V W X Y Z

I

i

J

j

K

k

Directions: Write as many letters as will fit on each line of these practice pages.

Name

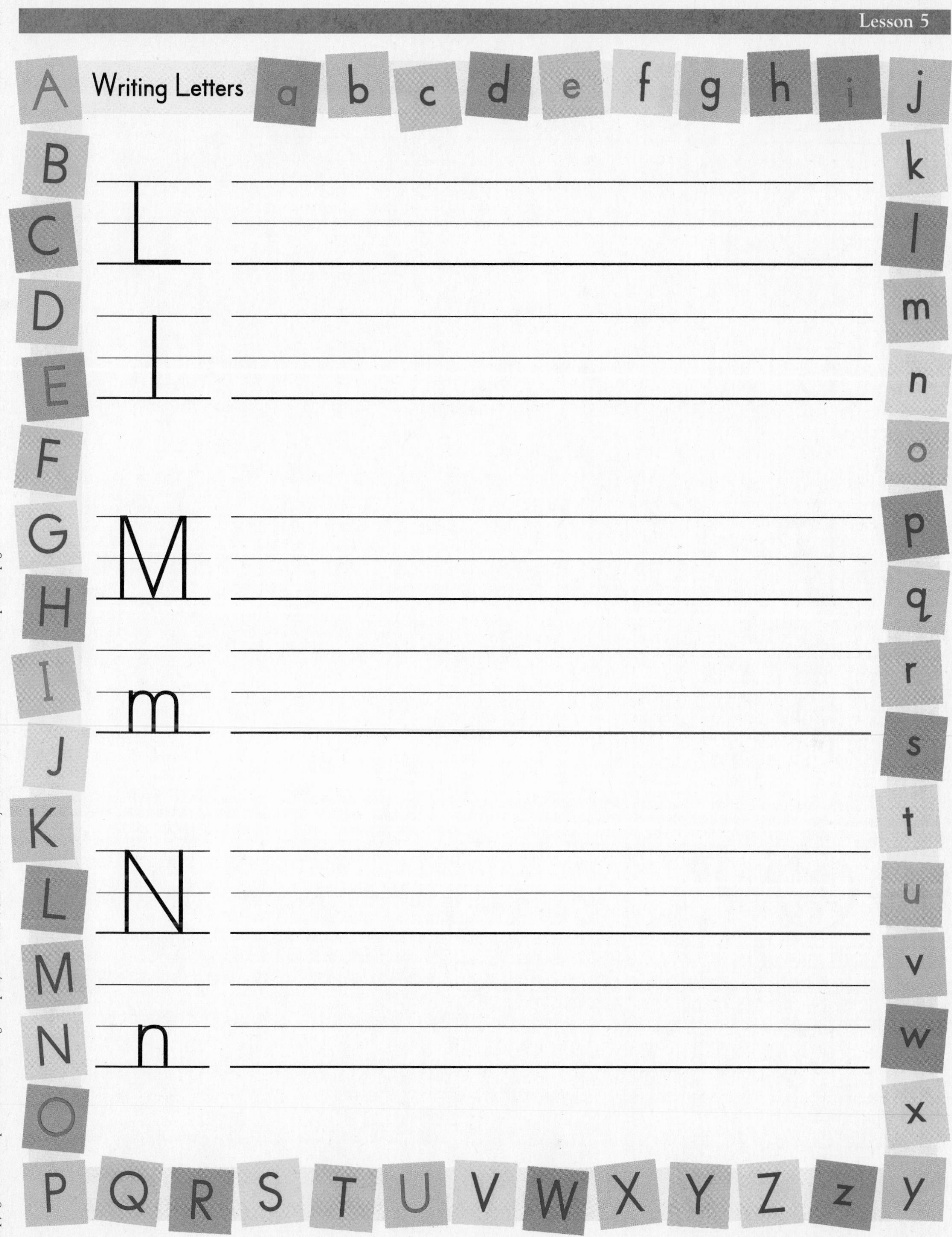

Writing Letters

L

l

M

m

N

n

Directions: Write as many letters as will fit on each line of these practice pages.

Letter Knowledge

Name

A Writing Letters a b c d e f g h i j

B k

O

C l

D m

o

E n

F o

P

G p

H q

p

I r

J s

K t

Q

L u

M v

q

N w

O x

P Q R S T U V W X Y Z z y

Directions: Write as many letters as will fit on each line of these practice pages.

Name

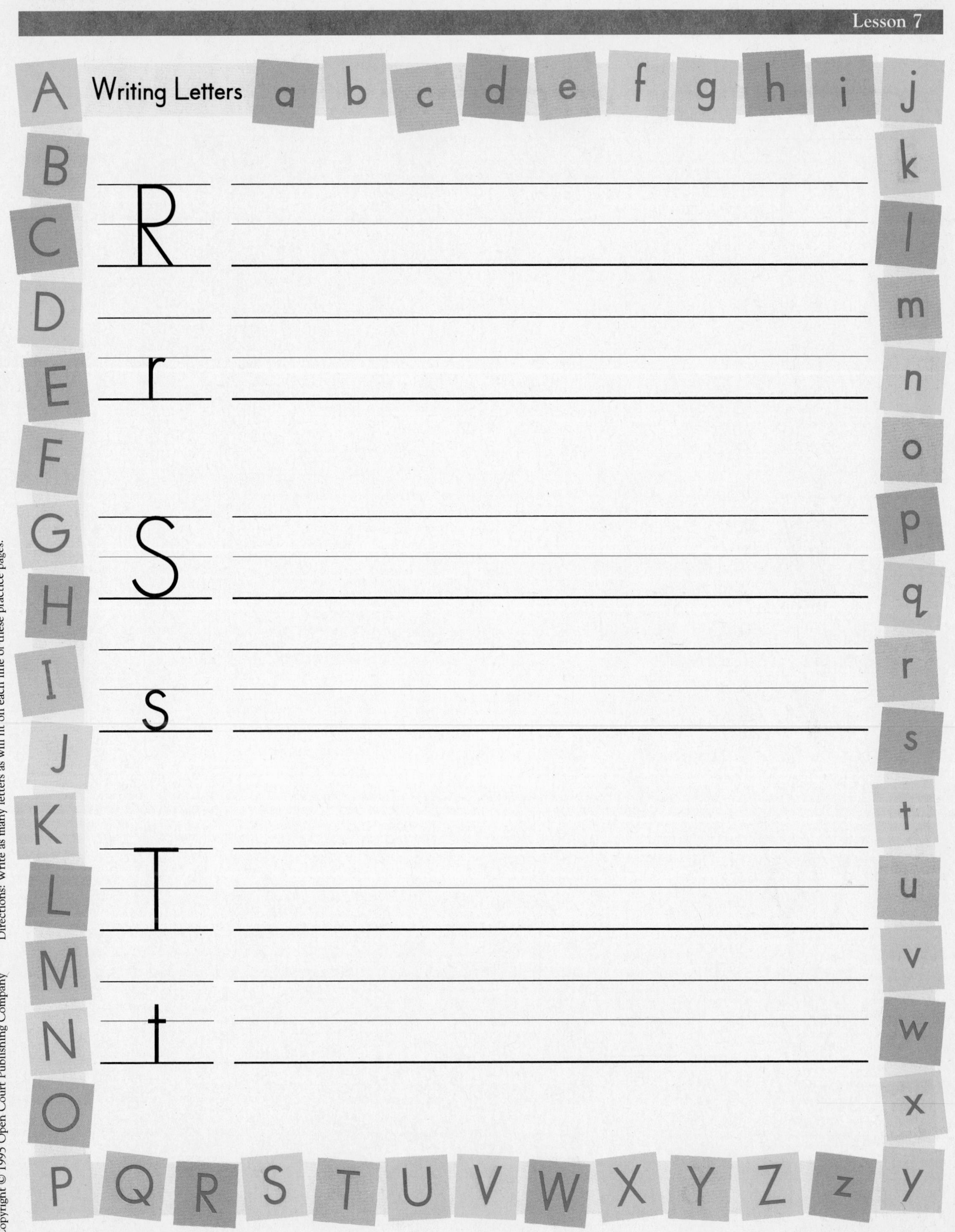

Writing Letters

R

r

S

s

T

t

Directions: Write as many letters as will fit on each line of these practice pages.

Letter Knowledge

Name

Writing Letters

U

u

V

v

W

w

Directions: Write as many letters as will fit on each line of these practice pages.

Name

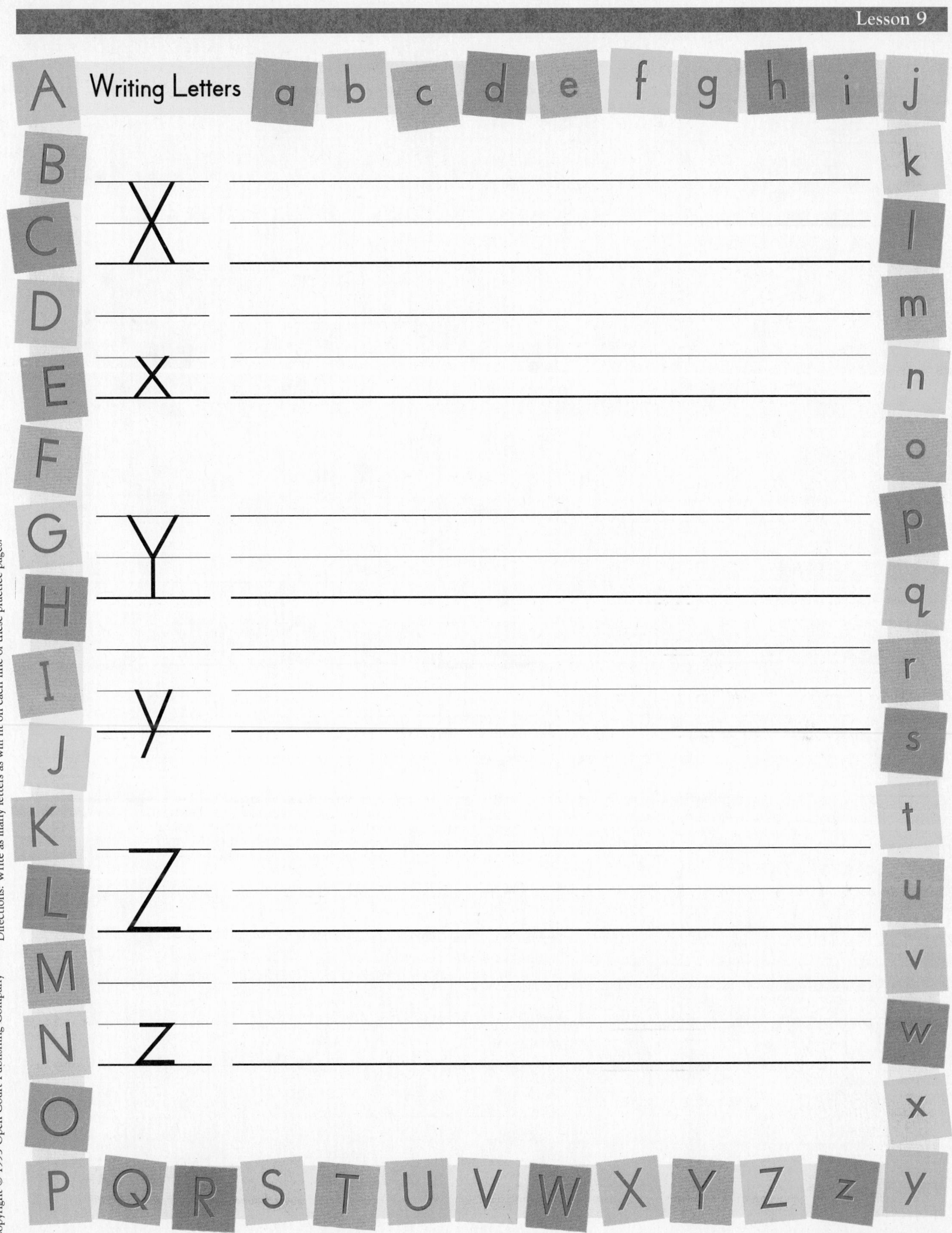

Directions: Write as many letters as will fit on each line of these practice pages.

Letter Knowledge

Name 3/22/10

Lesson 10

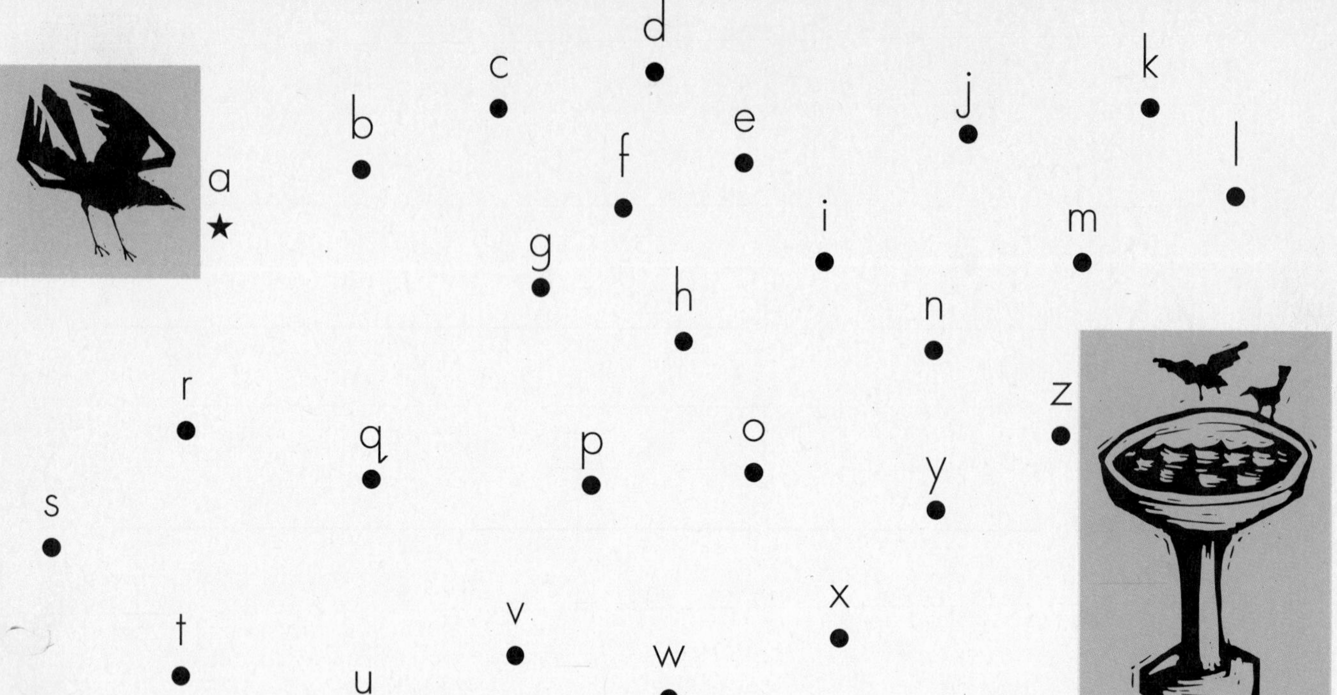

Directions: Connect the dots from *a* to *z*, then fill in the missing letters of the alphabet.

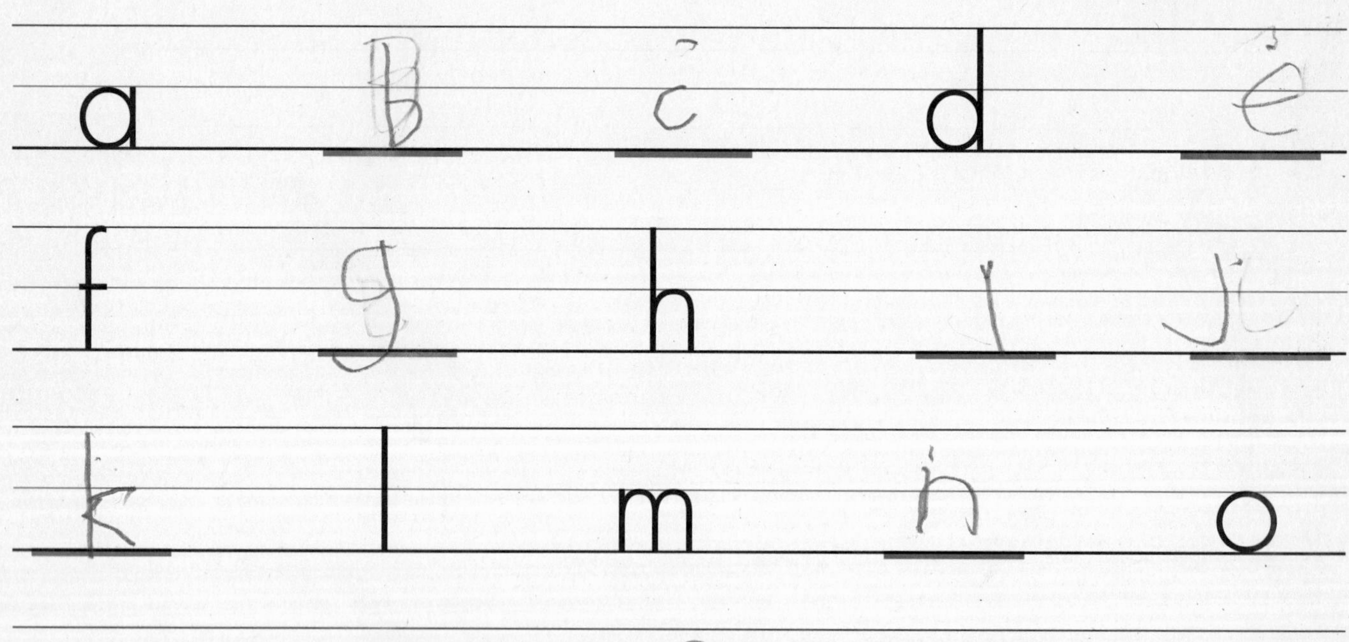

Name 3/22/10

B C A D E F G H I J K L M N O P Q R S T U V W X Y Z

A B C D E
F G H I J
K L M N O
P Q R S T
U V W X Y Z

Directions: Connect the dots from *a* to *z*, then fill in the missing letters of the alphabet.

Letter Knowledge

Name

Lesson 11

Sounds and Spellings

m

m

M

Directions: Practice writing *M* and *m*, then write *m* under each picture that has the /m/ sound.

Listening for Consonants

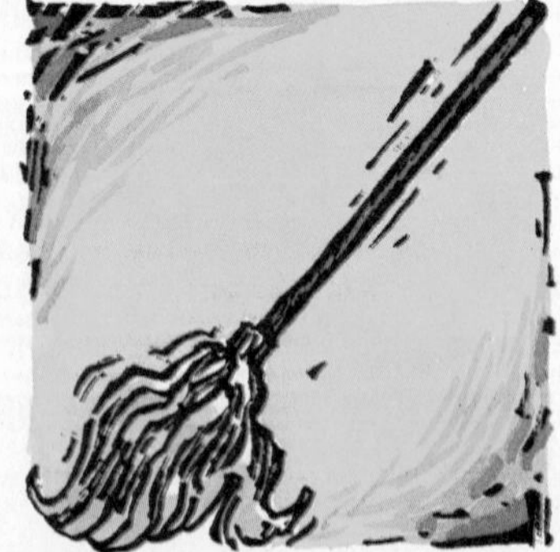

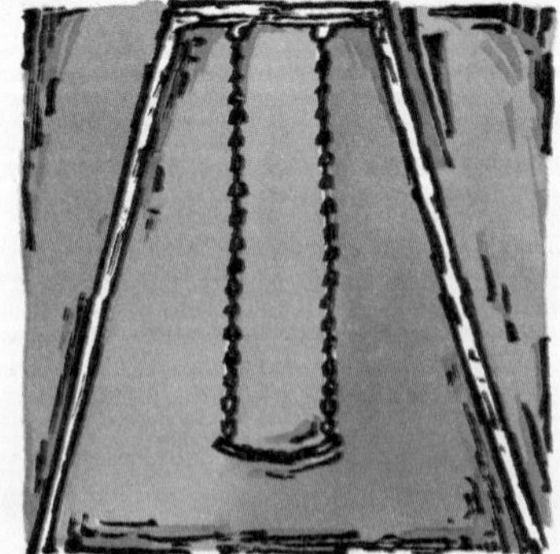

Name 3/25/10

Reading

I am on the 

I am in the 

I am a bird.  

I am in the 

I am on the 

I am a frog.  

I am on the 

I am in the 

I am a fish.  

Directions: Circle the correct picture to complete the sentence.

Decoding

Name

Lesson 13

Sounds and Spellings

t

t

T

Writing Words and Sentences

at

mat

I am at 

Directions: Practice writing t and T, then copy the words and finish the sentences.

Name

Listening for Consonants

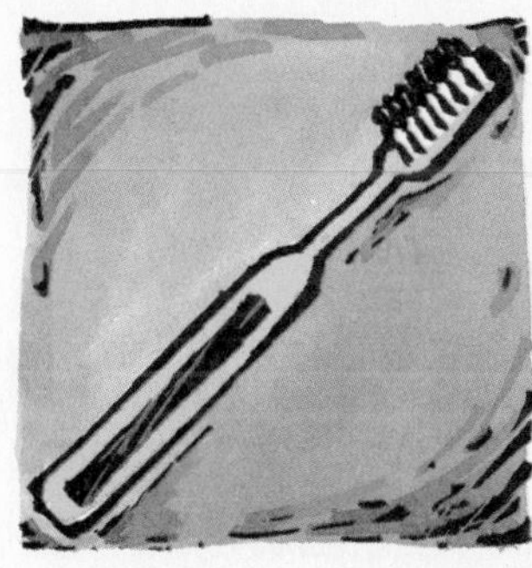

Directions: Write *t* on the first line if the picture begins with /t/ or write *t* on the second line if the picture ends with /t/.

Name

Sounds and Spellings

h_

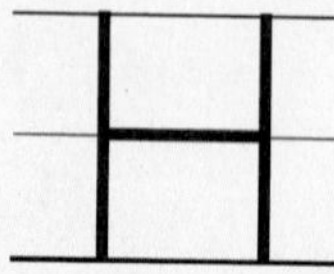

H

Completing Sentences

A tam is a ________.

Matt has a ________.

Directions: Practice writing *h* and *H*. Complete the sentences by writing words for the pictures.

Name

Listening for Consonants

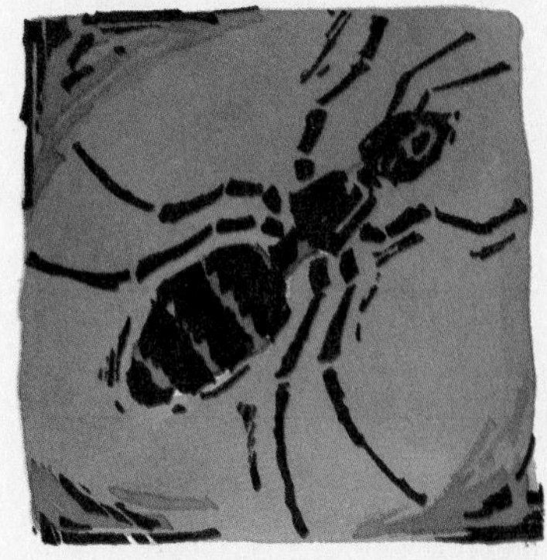

Directions: Write *h* under each picture whose name begins with /h/.

Name

Lesson 15

Sounds and Spellings

p

p

P

Writing Words and Sentences

pat

tap

Pam has a map.

Directions: Practice writing *p* and *P*, then copy the words and the sentence.

Name

Reading and Writing

Pat has a hat.

Pam is at the map.

I tap the hat.

Pat is on a mat.

I tap the mat.

Pat has a hat.

Directions: Choose the sentence that matches the picture and write that sentence in the space.

Name

Lesson 16

Sounds and Spellings

n

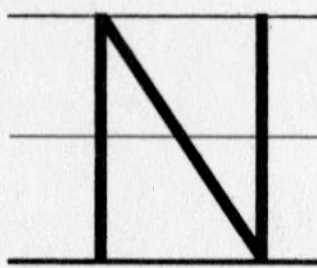

n

N

Writing Words and Sentences

nap

man

Nan has a nap.

Directions: Practice writing n and N, then copy the words and the sentence.

Name 4/28/10

Completing Sentences

I nap on a mat.

The man has a tam.

Pam has a hat.

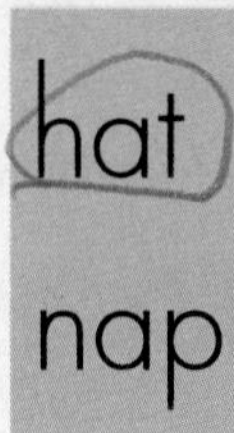

Pat has a map.

The ant is on the ham.

Nat has a pan.

Directions: Look at the pictures and finish the sentences with the appropriate words.

Name

Sounds and Spellings

c

c

C

Writing Words and Sentences

cat

cap

Can the cat tap on the can?

Directions: Practice writing c and C, then copy the words and the sentence.

Name

Writing Words

Drawing

The hats are on the cats.

Directions: Write the pictured words in the spaces provided, then draw a picture that matches the sentence.

Blending/Decoding

Name

Lesson 20

Sounds and Spellings

i

i

I

Writing Words and Sentences

him tips

Tim sits in the sand.

Directions: Practice writing *i* and *I*, then copy the words and the sentence.

Name

Writing and Reading

Directions: Write the sound represented by each Sound/Spelling Card picture to form a word.

Blending

Name

Writing Words

Directions: Choose the word that matches each picture, and write the word in the space provided.

pin map stamp mints picnic cap

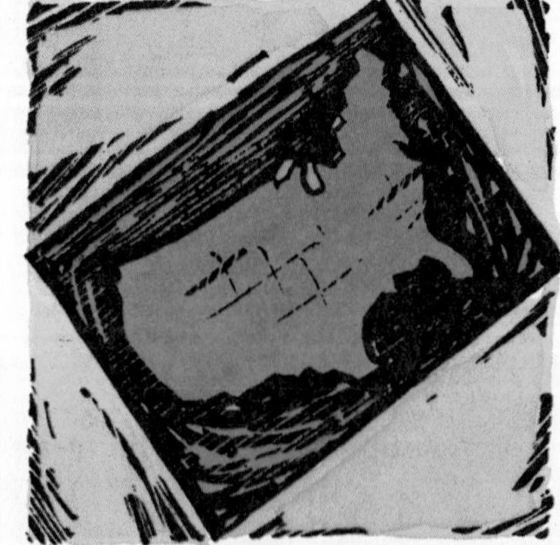

Name

Completing Sentences

Sid ____________ a handstand.

did
dad

Nan sat on the ____________.

hit
hat

Sam has a ____________.

pin
pan

Directions: Look at the pictures and finish the sentences with the appropriate words.

Decoding

Name

Sounds and Spellings

b

b

B

Writing Words and Sentences

bib bands

A bat was a bit sad.

Directions: Practice writing *b* and *B*, then copy the words and the sentences.

Name

Reading and Writing

bat

bats

bit

pin

pit

pan

Sid sat in the sand.

Nan and Min had a picnic.

Directions: Write the word that matches each picture, then write the sentence represented by the picture.

Name

Sounds and Spellings

r

r

R

Writing Words and Sentences

rip

trip

A rat bit the cat and ran.

Directions: Practice writing r and R, then copy the words and the sentence.

Name

Reading and Writing

Brad ran on the ramp.

The rabbit is in the crib.

Min ran at camp.

Tim is on a trip.

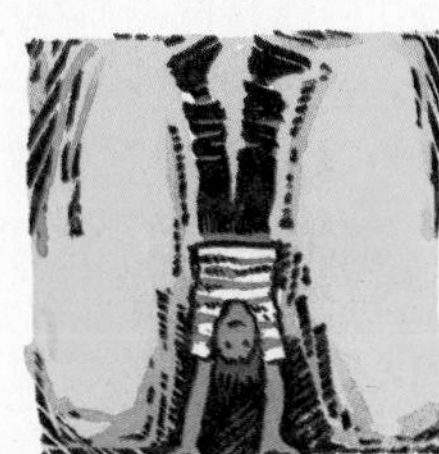

Sid stands in the sand.

Sid can stand on his hands.

Directions: Copy the sentence that matches each picture.

Blending

Name

Sounds and Spellings

f

f

F

Writing Words and Sentences

fan

fat

Can the fat cat fit in the hat?

Directions: Practice writing *f* and *F*, then copy the words and the sentence.

Name

Writing and Reading

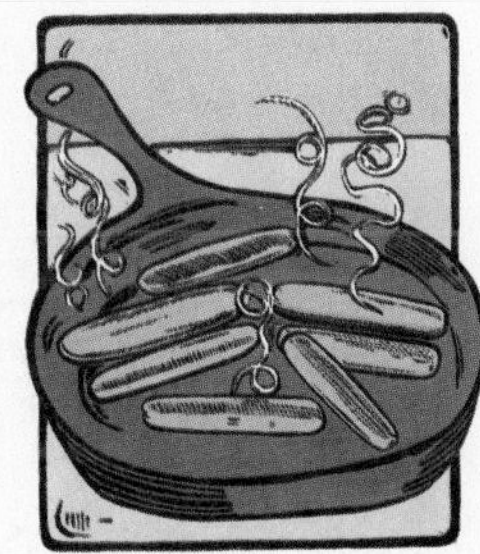

Directions: Write the letter represented by each Sound/Spelling Card picture to form a word.

Blending

Name

Lesson 25

Sounds and Spellings

g

g

G

Writing Words and Sentences

gas grab

The pig is big.

Directions: Practice writing *g* and *G*; then copy the words and the sentence.

Name

Writing Words

pig
sag
grin

tag
dig
big

Directions: Write the words represented in the picture, then write a third word with the /g/ sound that is in the picture.

Name

Lesson 26

Listening for Vowels

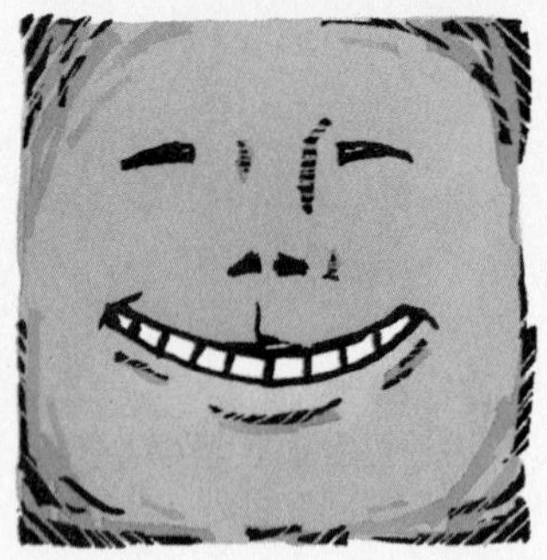

__i__ __a__

Directions: Write the name of each picture beneath the *i* or *a* depending on the short vowel sound in the word.

Name

Writing Words

cabin
hatpin
rabbit

Completing Sentences

Dad ________ the cat.

fins
fans

The pig can ________ in the bag.

fat
fit

Directions: Write the matching word next to each picture, then finish the sentences with the appropriate word.

Name

Lesson 27

Sounds and Spellings

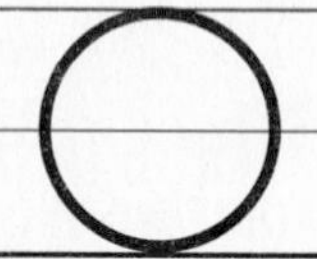

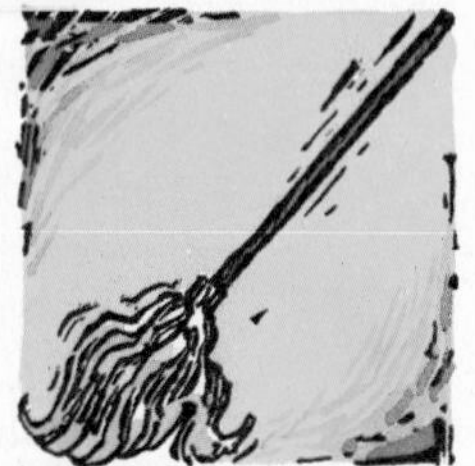

The dog can stop the top.

Directions: Practice writing *o* and O, then write the word that matches each picture and copy the sentence.

Name

Reading and Writing

Dad can spin a ________.

tip
top
tap

Pam and Sam ________ the pig.

pit
pot
pat

Dictation and Spelling

Directions: Finish the sentences with the appropriate word.

Decoding/Spelling

Name

Sounds and Spellings

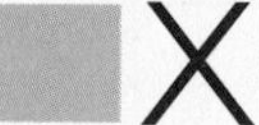

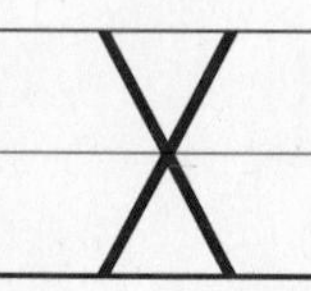

X

Writing Words and Sentences

fox

mix

The ax is in the box.

Directions: Practice writing *x* and *X*, then copy the words and the sentence.

Name

Listening for Vowels

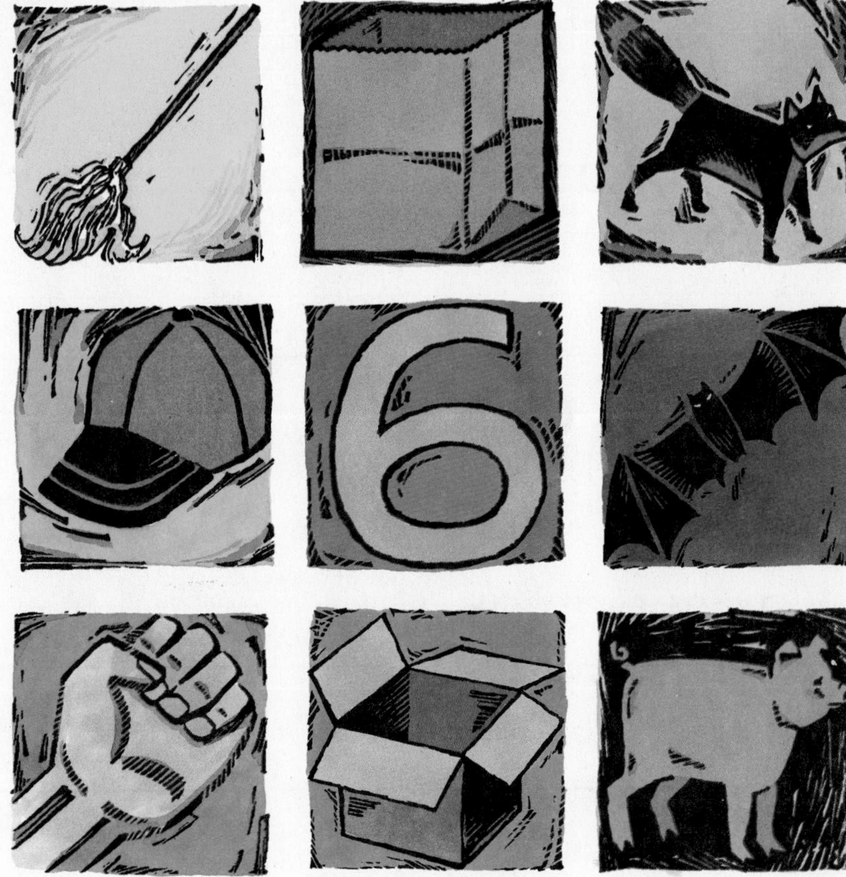

_i_   _a_   _o_

Directions: Write the name of each picture beneath the short vowel spelling contained in that word.

Name

Reading and Writing

The fox sat on the mat.

The fox has six ants.

An ax is in the box.

Max has an ax.

The cat was in the mix.

The cat sits in the box.

Dad can fix the map.

Dan taps the mix.

Name

Writing Words

frog
pan
box

Dictation and Spelling

Directions: Copy the words represented in the picture, then write a third word that is also in the picture.

Name

Sounds and Spellings

ar

Directions: Write the /ar/ word next to each picture, then copy the sentence.

Writing Words and Sentences

The car is in the barn.

Name

Writing Words

farm

star

ram

barn

man

rabbit

frog

ax

Directions: Look at the picture, write the words that appear in the picture, then name other objects in the picture. Circle the words with the /ar/ sound.

Blending

Name

Sounds and Spellings

c

■ck

Writing Words

s st p r sn d tr

_ack _ick _ock

Directions: Form words by blending the initial consonants in the green box with _ack, _ick, and _ock.

Name

Reading and Writing Sentences

Rick has socks in the sack.
Pat picks a stick in the stack.

Dictation and Spelling

Directions: Write the sentence that describes the picture.

Decoding/Spelling

Name

Sounds and Spellings

u

Writing Words and Sentences

bug

drum

The duck is stuck in the mud.

Directions: Practice writing *u* and *U*, then copy the words and the sentence.

Name

Reading and Writing Sentences

She scrubs the pup's rug.

She hugs the pup.

Bud dug in the sun.

The bug runs up the pump.

It is fun to scrub the tub.

She drops her duck in the tub.

Directions: Copy the sentence that describes each picture.

Name

Sounds and Spellings

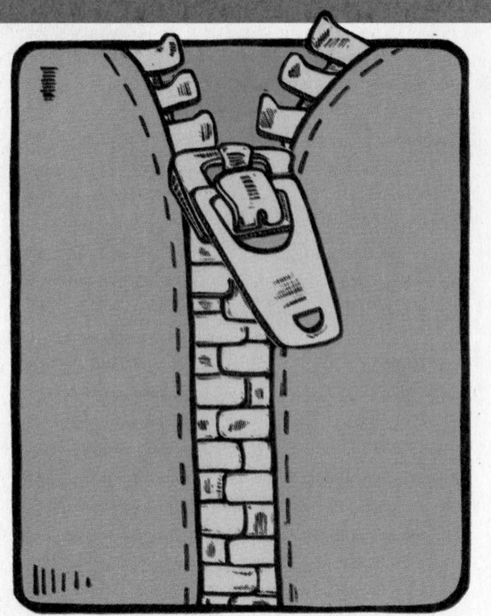

z

z

Z

Writing Words and Sentences

zip buzz

The bug ran in a zigzag.

Directions: Practice writing z and Z, then copy the words and the sentence.

Name

Reading and Writing Sentences

Lil fills the pickle jar.
Liz has lots of dolls.

Dictation and Spelling

Directions: Write the sentence that describes the picture.

Name

Sounds and Spellings

e

E

Writing Words and Sentences

hen   tent

neck   sled

The egg fell on the bed.

Directions: Practice writing e and E, then copy the words and the sentence.

Name

Writing Words

Directions: Label each picture, complete the sentence, and write the spelling represented by each Sound/Spelling Card picture at the bottom of the page to form a word.

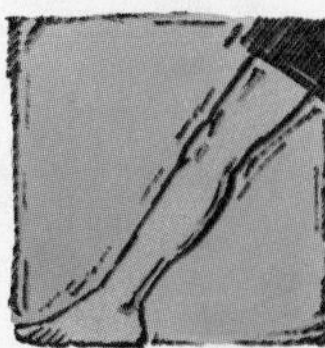

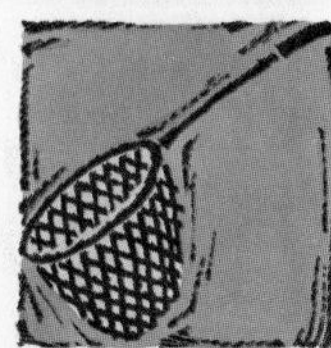

An insect has __________ legs.

Name ______________________

Lesson 37

Completing Sentences

instead head bread fed dead

Directions: Finish each sentence with the appropriate word.

1. Ted has ______________ for a snack.

2. "The bug is ______________," said Meg.

3. Greg ______________ the red hen.

4. Peg ran ______________ of Ben.

5. Can you fix the puppet's ______________?

Name

Writing Words

left bed instead bread nest

Dictation and Spelling

Directions: Write the word that matches each picture.

Name

Sounds and Spellings

y__

y

Y

Writing Words and Sentences

yam

yes

yell

yet

The cat has yards of yarn.

Directions: Practice writing y and Y, then copy the words and the sentence.

Name

Reading and Writing Sentences

1.  2. 3.

The dog yelps at the rabbit.
A rabbit nibbles plants in the yard.
The dog naps in the backyard.

1. ____________________

2. ____________________

3. ____________________

Directions: Write the sentence that matches each picture in the correct order.

Decoding

Name

Sounds and Spellings

w_

w

W

Writing Words and Sentences

wet

wag

wiggle

well

Will you get a wagon?

Directions: Practice writing *w* and W, then copy the words and the sentence.

Name

Sounds and Spellings

wh_

when

whiz

Dictation and Spelling

Directions: Copy the words with the /hw/ sound in the spaces provided.

Name

Sounds and Spellings

Directions: Copy the words and the sentence in the spaces provided.

Writing Words and Sentences

her

bird

girl

sister

curl

turn

Bert had a hamburger for supper.

Name

Unscrambling Sentences

has girl a
The turtle. little

nest. bird sits on
purple a The

Directions: Unscramble the words to form a sentence that describes the picture.

Name

Lesson 41

Word Study

Directions: Fill in each blank with a vowel to form a word.

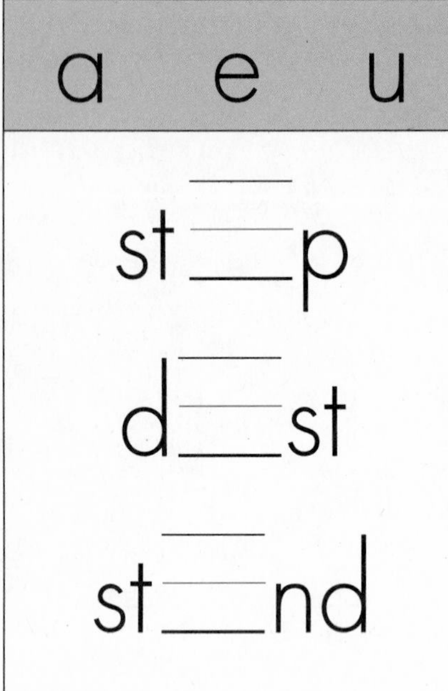

a i o

d___p

p___nd

l___nd

e i o

t___p

br___ck

b___st

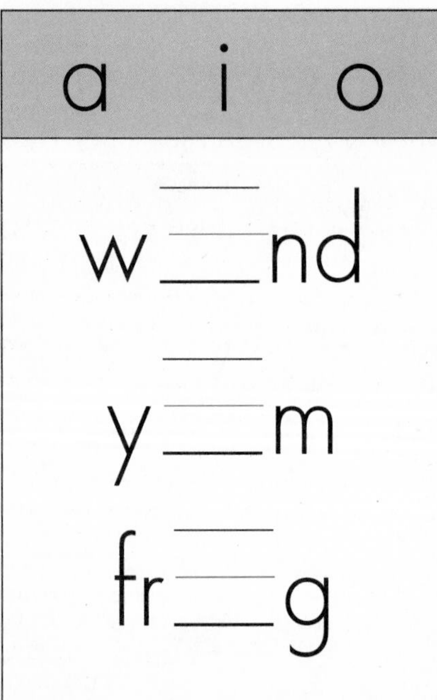

e o u

b___g

dr___p

h___lp

i o u

l___ck

f___n

t___b

Discriminating Short Vowels

Name

Completing Sentences

1. Sam had bread and ______________.

better
butter

2. Mom ______________ the car.

stepped
stopped

3. Herb ______________ his bag.

packed
pecked

4. The girls ______________ in the dirt.

dig
dog

Dictation and Spelling

Directions: Finish each sentence with the appropriate word.

Name

Sounds and Spellings

sh

Writing Words and Sentences

shop shack

wish crash

sharp flash

Sherman has six shells in a box.

Directions: Copy the words and the sentence in the spaces provided.

Name

Lesson 42

Writing Words

dish ship shirt fresh shell brush fish

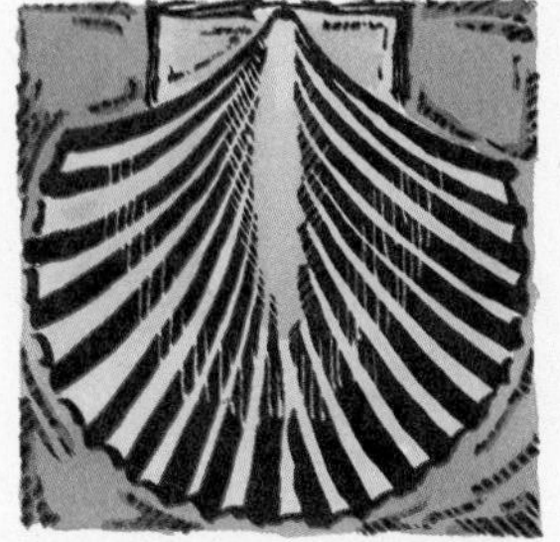

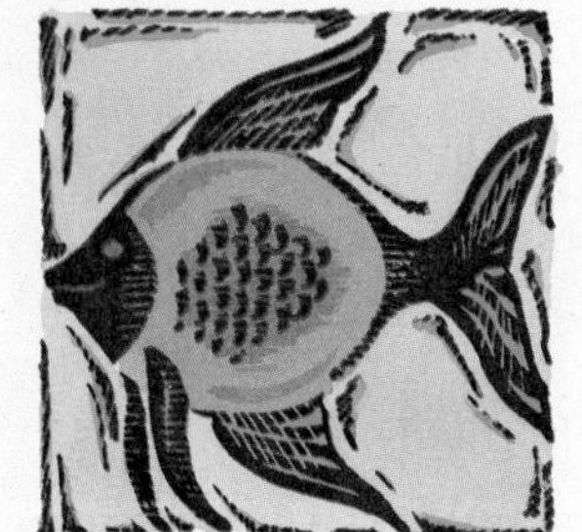

Directions: Match each word to the appropriate picture, then write the spelling represented by each Sound/Spelling Card picture to form a word at the bottom.

Decoding

Name

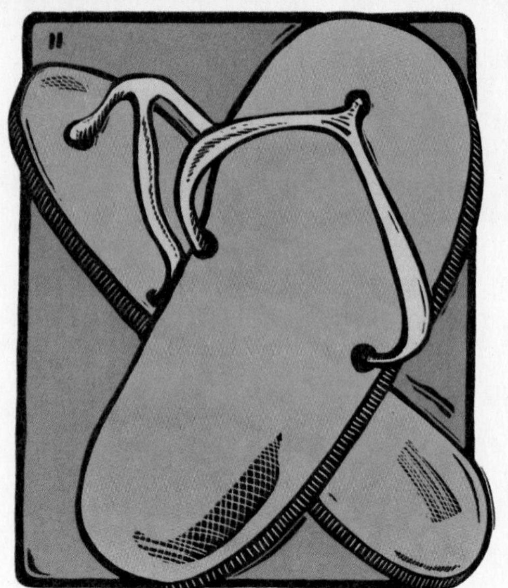

Sounds and Spellings

th

Writing Words and Sentences

thick that

with bath

thunder

This is a thin twig.

Directions: Copy the words and the sentence in the spaces provided.

Name

Unscrambling Sentences

bird feathers. This red has

Dictation and Spelling

Directions: Unscramble the words to form a sentence that describes the picture.

Name

Sounds and Spellings

ch

Writing Words and Sentences

chin

church

chick

inch

chill

bunch

The children munch on chips.

Directions: Copy the words and the sentence in the spaces provided.

Name

Writing Words

check chop chimp chicken
ranch bench much lunchbox

Directions: Match each word to the appropriate picture, then write a sentence using the words in the box.

Decoding

Name

Sounds and Spellings

ch

■tch

Writing Words and Sentences

fetch ________ switch ________

itch ________ stretch ________

Mitch catches the pitch.

____

Stitch a patch on the cap.

____

Directions: Copy the words and the sentences in the spaces provided.

Name

Writing Words

fetch patches crutches catch ditch scratch

Dictation and Spelling

Directions: Match a word to each picture.

Decoding/Spelling

Name

Lesson 46

Completing Sentences

Directions: Finish each sentence with the appropriate words.

split strip splash strap splinter scratches

1. The frog went into the water with a ______.

2. Max has a ______ in his hand.

3. The carpenter cut a thin ______ of plastic.

4. The dog ______ its back.

Name

Reading

Patches and Dan

1. Dan pitches the stick.
2. Patches wants to catch it.
3. The stick splashes in the pond.
4. Patches fetches the stick.

____

____

____

____

Directions: Number each picture to match the sentence it describes.

Blending

Name

Lesson 47

Sounds and Spellings

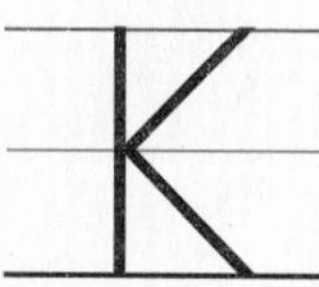

K

Writing Words and Sentences

kick

bark

kitchen

silk

The kitten laps milk.

Directions: Practice writing *k* and K, then copy the words and the sentence.

Name

Writing Words

park kept breakfast mask kick kettle

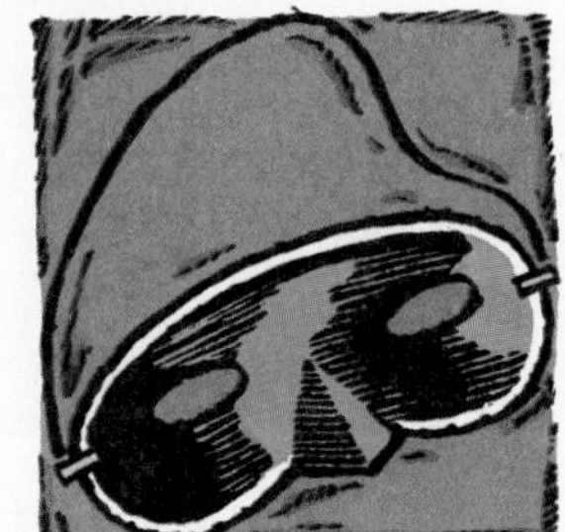

Dictation and Spelling

Directions: Match a word to each picture.

Name

Lesson 48

Sounds and Spellings

a

a_e

Writing Words and Sentences

apron

ape

table

shape

cradle

skate

Dave made a mask with paper and tape.

Directions: Copy the words and the sentence in the spaces provided.

Name

Completing Sentences

1. Ted has a ____________ on his head.

cap
cape

2. Pat fixed his model ____________.

plan
plane

3. A whale ____________ swim.

can
cane

4. Mark ____________ muffins.

mad
made

5. Kate has a ____________ kitten.

fat
fate

Directions: Finish each sentence with the appropriate word.

Name

Sounds and Spellings

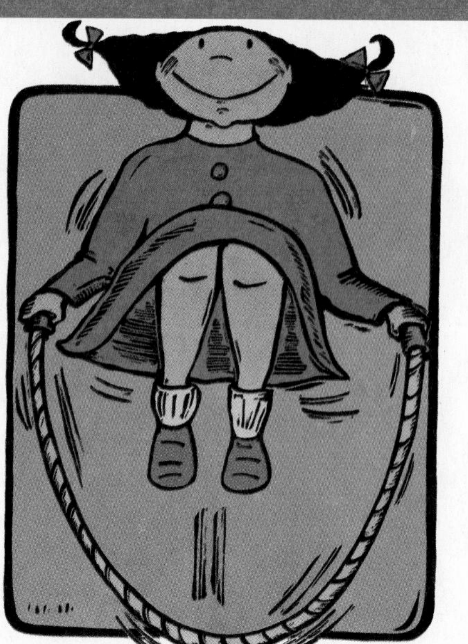

j

J

Writing Words and Sentences

job juggle

judge badge

Jake cut the tall hedge.

Directions: Practice writing j and J, then copy the words and the sentence.

Name

Jack's dad jogs across the bridge.

Jan jumps across the ditch.

Dictation and Spelling

Directions: Copy the sentence that matches the picture.

Name

Directions: Copy the words and the sentence in the spaces provided.

Sounds and Spellings

j ge

■dge gi_

Writing Words and Sentences

gem ______ ginger ______

page ______ stage ______

The gerbil ran into the cage.

Name

Lesson 50

Listening for Consonant Sounds

gag judge bridge game
gentle bag grip badge

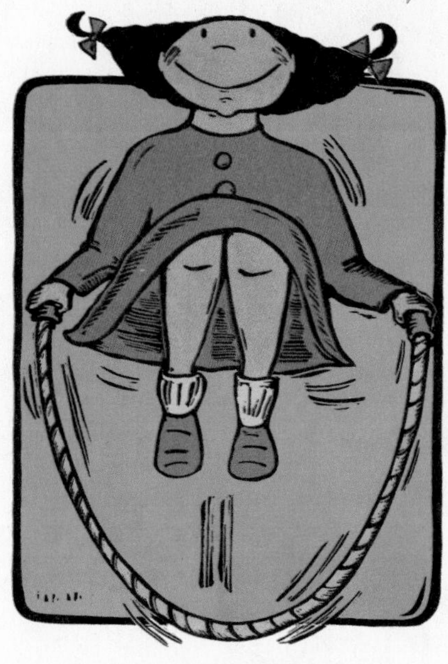

Directions: List each word under the Sound/Spelling Card picture for /j/ or /g/.

Decoding

Name

Sounds and Spellings

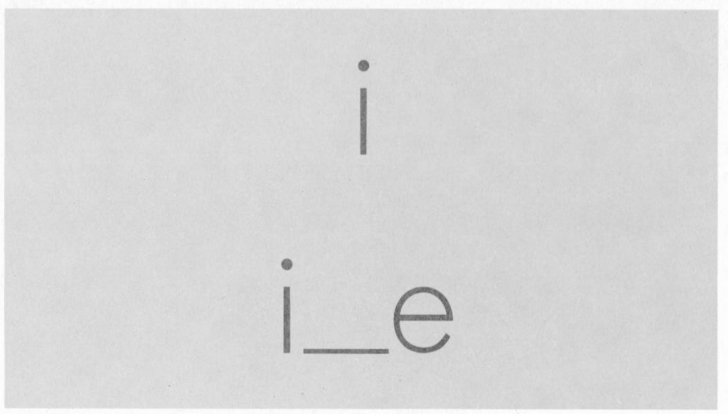

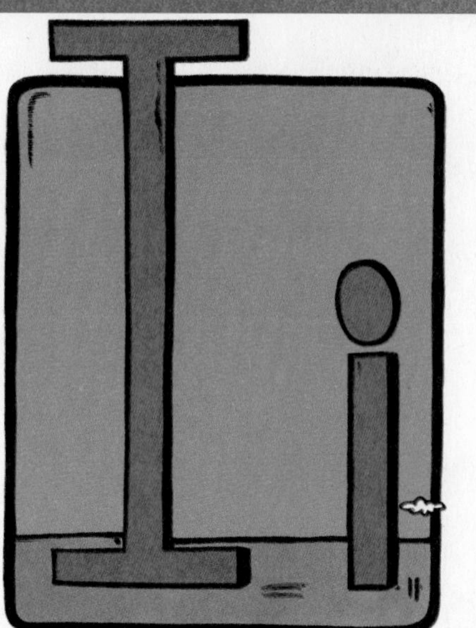

Writing Words and Sentences

tiger ____________ title ____________

time ____________ smile ____________

Nine fish swim in the tide.

____

Did you find the dime?

____

Name

Completing Sentences

1. I like to ____________ a bike. | rid / ride

2. Did you ____________ the page? | rip / ripe

3. Dad made a ____________ dinner. | fin / fine

4. The man was gentle and ____________. | kin / kind

Dictation and Spelling

Directions: Complete each sentence with the appropriate word.

Name

Directions: Copy the words and the sentences in the spaces provided.

Sounds and Spellings

s

ce

ci_

Writing Words and Sentences

cent

circus

space

cider

Grace likes nice mice.

We danced in a circle.

Name

Listening for Consonant Sounds

face cake ice candle picnic
carrot cider twice circle

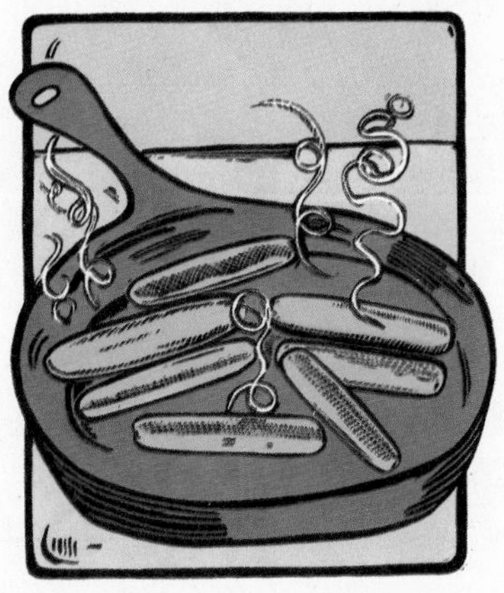

Directions: List each word under the Sound/Spelling Card picture for /s/ or /k/.

Name

Lesson 53

Writing Opposites

last finished soft off

1. The girl started the race. ____________

2. Dad turned the lamp on. ____________

3. Linda is first in line. ____________

4. The bed is too hard. ____________

Writing Synonyms

little ran cut

1. Dad will trim the hedge. ____________

2. Is a gerbil small? ____________

3. Kate raced up the hill. ____________

Directions: Write the word that means the opposite of the underlined word on the top half of the page, then write the word that is almost the same as the underlined word on the bottom half.

Name

Writing Rhyming Words

line mile ice cent

Dictation and Spelling

Directions: Choose the word that rhymes with each picture and write it on the space provided.

Name

Sounds and Spellings

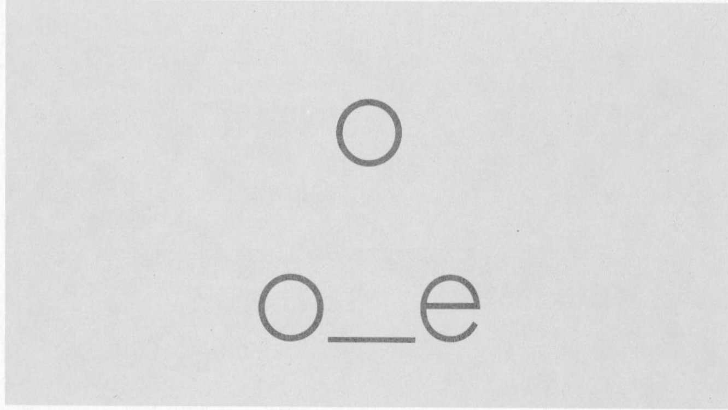

Writing Words and Sentences

no

hold

broke

stone

The dog hid the bone.

I told him to go home.

Name

Listening for Words

○ April ○ open ○ oval	○ hop ○ hope ○ hold	○ block ○ bone ○ broke
○ acorn ○ apple ○ able	○ not ○ nice ○ notes	○ spoke ○ spot ○ spike

An octopus has ______ bones.

 ______

 ______

Directions: Mark each word according to the clues given. Complete the sentence using the letters represented in the pictures.

Decoding

Name

Sounds and Spellings

z

_s

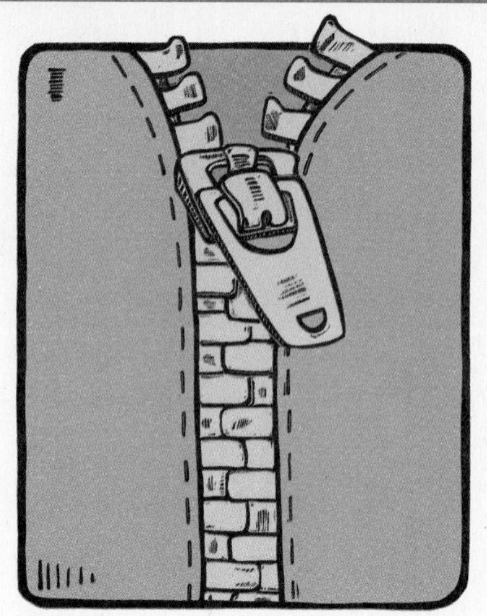

Writing Words

nose

eggs

chips rose this has mice pins

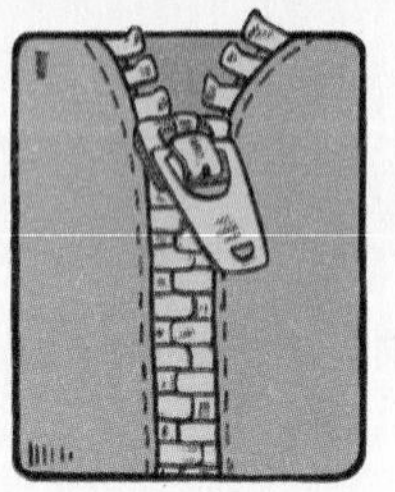

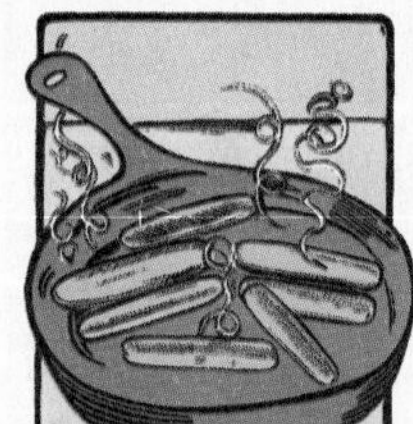

Directions: Copy the two words, then list the words in the green box under the Sound/Spelling Card picture for /z/ or /s/.

Name

Writing Opposites

open no white close yes black

Dictation and Spelling

Directions: Write the pairs of opposite words next to each other.

Name

Sounds and Spellings

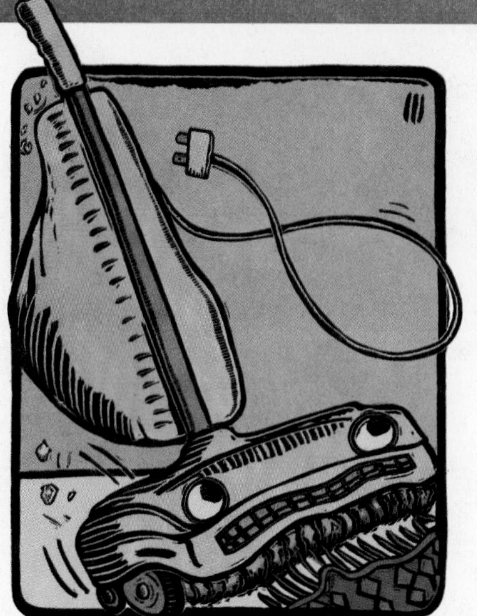

v

v

V

Directions: Practice writing *v* and V, then copy the words and the sentence.

Writing Words and Sentences

vine van

brave five

Vince has seven valentines.

Name

Reading and Writing Sentences

The mule has a cute hat.

The mule licks an ice cube.

Dictation and Spelling

Directions: Write the sentence described by the picture.

Name

Sounds and Spellings

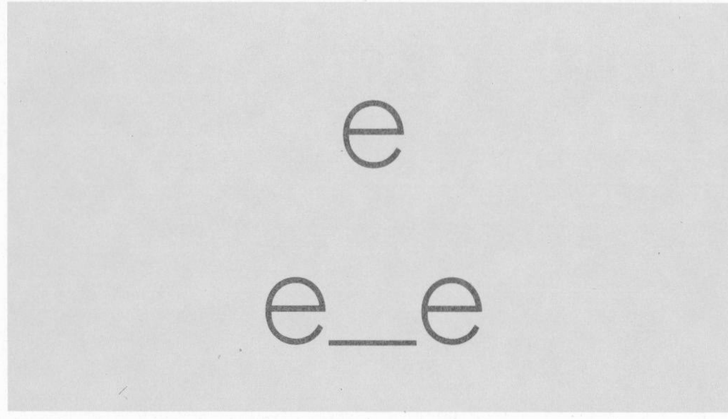

Writing Words and Sentences

she

these

even

me

Pete sits here.

Steve had a fever.

Directions: Copy the words and the sentences in the spaces provided.

Name

Reading and Writing

The giraffe has a huge neck.

Eve pets the giraffe.

The man is on skates.

The man is on the trapeze.

We sat on the fence.

Put a dime in the meter.

Directions: Write the sentence described by each picture.

Name

Lesson 59

Listening for Vowels

cake cape cap

help here hen

kitchen kitten kite

rope robber rocket

cute cub cube

crane crash crate

trapeze tape tap

Directions: Choose the word with a different vowel sound from the others in each group, and write it on the space provided.

Name

Word Study

cap
cake
make

bike
kitten
kite

cube
cute
cut

nose
hose
rose

Dictation and Spelling

Directions: Write the word described by each picture.

Name

Lesson 60

Sounds and Spellings

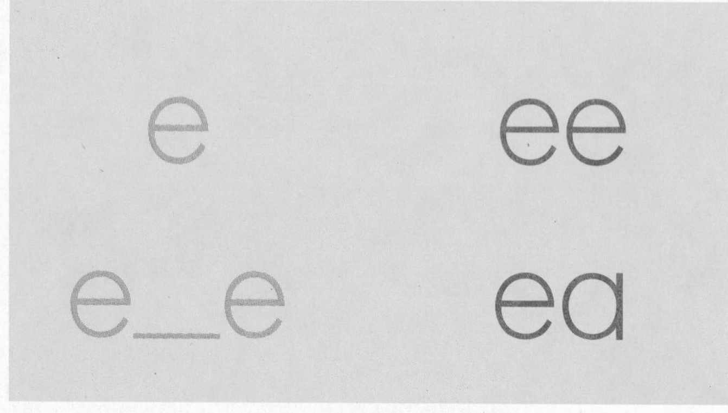

Writing Words and Sentences

eagle

meal

feel

sheep

Steve eats green beans.

The sneakers fit his feet.

Name

Writing Opposites

begin awake fake far real remember
end forget freeze near melt asleep

Directions: Write the pairs of opposite words next to each other.

Antonyms

Name

Sounds and Spellings

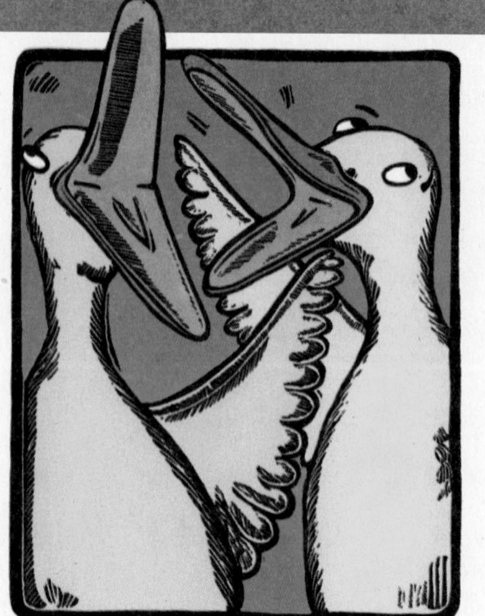

qu_

qu Qu

Writing Words and Sentences

queen quack

quiet quit

The quilt is made of squares.

Name

Reading and Writing Sentences

The lily is white.

The lilies are white.

The box is shiny.

The box is dirty.

Dictation and Spelling

Directions: Write the sentence described by each picture.

Decoding/Spelling

Name

Lesson 64

Writing Synonyms

tiny funny muddy unhappy

dirty ____________ silly ____________

little ____________ sad ____________

Listening for Words

○ water ○ winter ○ whisper	○ grass ○ glass ○ grab	○ story ○ stories ○ study
○ dirty ○ dizzy ○ distance	○ quack ○ quake ○ quick	○ sheep ○ shore ○ shape

Directions: Write each word next to its synonym, then choose the correct word in each box based on the clues given.

Name

Word Study

ponies thirsty twenty
emergency stories cherries

1. Popcorn can make you ________________.

2. Call 911 in an ________________.

3. Jerry likes to eat red ________________.

4. Thirty is more than ________________.

5. The ________________ were nice to ride.

6. There are many ________________ to read in the library.

Directions: Finish each sentence with the appropriate word.

Name

Lesson 65

Sounds and Spellings

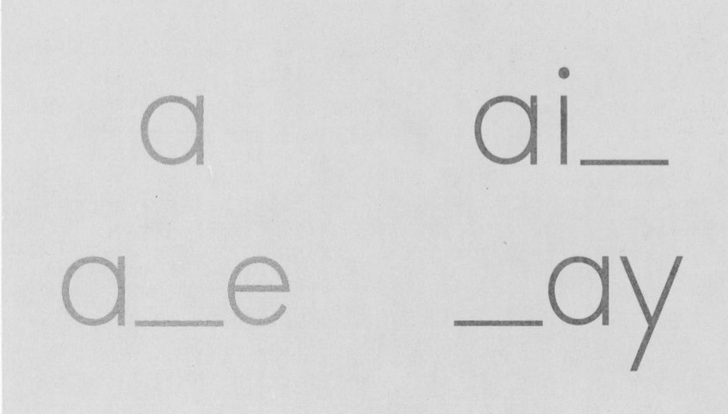

Directions: Copy the words and the sentences in the spaces provided.

Writing Words and Sentences

pail

snail

pay

stay

The raisins are stale.

Kay's birthday is in May.

Name

Homophones

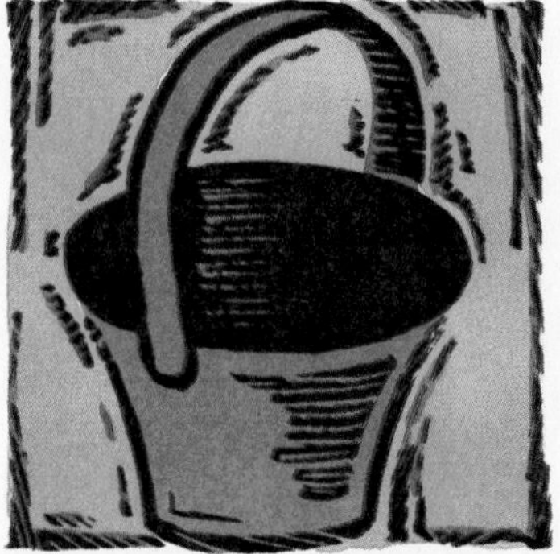

pale pail

sail sale

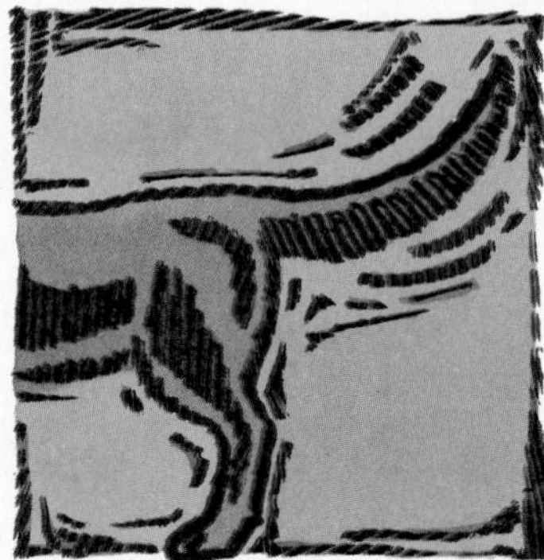

tale tail

Dictation and Spelling

Directions: Write the homophone that matches each picture.

Decoding/Spelling

Name

Sounds and Spellings

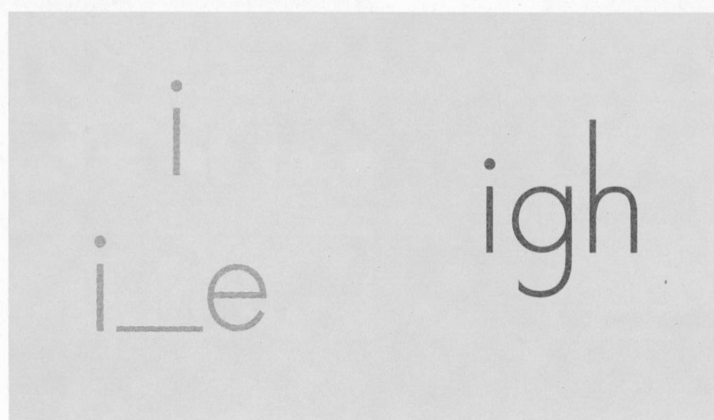

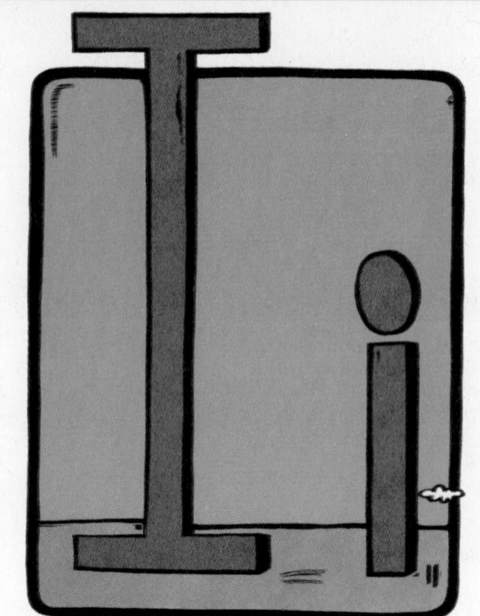

Writing Words and Sentences

high
sigh
sight
flight

The light is bright.

You might be right.

Directions: Copy the words and the sentences in the spaces provided.

Name

Writing Compound Words

light	light
night	chair
high	rope
tight	bulb

Completing Sentences

1. The baby eats in the ______.

2. I saw a ______ walker.

3. The lamp needs a ______.

4. Ben sleeps with a ______.

Directions: Choose one word from each column to form a compound word, then use each word to finish the sentences.

Name

Sounds and Spellings

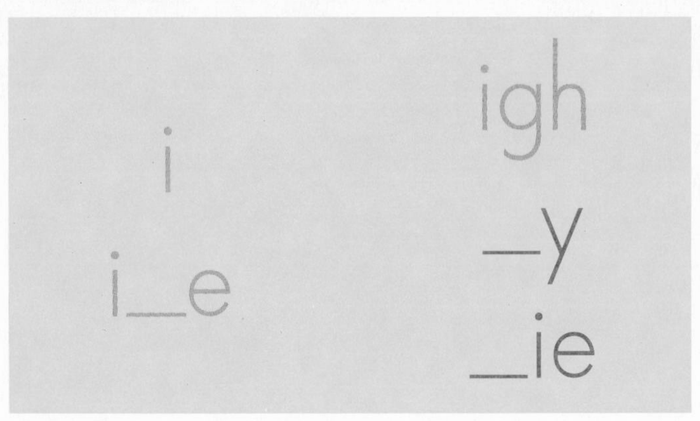

Writing Words and Sentences

try

tries

fly

flies

The kite flies in the sky.

Try the apple pie.

Name

Completing Sentences

fly tie tries pie sky

1. The ________ buzzes by my head.

2. I ate the cherry ________ all by myself.

3. Tyrone ________ to do a trick.

Dictation and Spelling

 Directions: Finish each sentence with the appropriate word.

Decoding/Spelling

Name

Sounds and Spellings

Writing Words and Sentences

wing

thing

ring

spring

The king rang a gong.

We sang a long song.

Directions: Copy the words and the sentences in the spaces provided.

Name

Reading and Writing

The string is tangled.

The string is in a box.

Hank plays ping pong.

Hank plays the tape.

Listening for Words

○ hung ○ hang ○ hinge	○ skunk ○ snake ○ snap	○ string ○ strong ○ stripe
○ seed ○ sing ○ sweet	○ more ○ mole ○ most	○ cry ○ cries ○ cried

Directions: Write the sentence described by each picture, then choose the correct word based on the clues given.

Name

Add -ing

Directions: Match the rhyming words, adding *-ing* to the word written in each space.

hop	jump	sing	run	think
smile	dig	hope	hide	eat

ring ____________ fig ____________

feet ____________ fun ____________

mop ____________ soap ____________

bump ____________ ride ____________

file ____________ sink ____________

Blending

Name

Completing Sentences

1. Melissa is ____________.

2. A dog is ____________.

3. Sam is ____________.

4. The girl is ____________.

Dictation and Spelling

Directions: Choose from the words from the green box on page 128 and add *-ng* to finish each sentence.

Name

Lesson 70

Completing Sentences

Directions: Finish each sentence with the appropriate word.

1. I ____________ I'll play a tape.

   think   thing

2. Fred put on his ____________.

   soaks   socks

3. That's a big ____________ of paper.

   stack   stake

4. This is a ____________ cat.

   cut   cute

5. We ____________ with the music.

   sing   song

6. Tom has ____________ feet.

   muddy   many

Blending

Name

Adding -ed and -ing

paint

bake

slip

rule

Writing Synonyms

song nice road cute

pretty

kind

music

highway

Directions: Add *-ed* and *-ing* to each word, then write the new words in the spaces provided. Match the synonyms at the bottom of the page.

Outlaw Words

a
an
are
away
climb
come
could
do
does
eight
eyes
for
four
guess
half
have
heard
hurray
lived
Mr.
of
oh
once
one
out
pull
said
says
seven
should
show
the
they
thing
to
today
too
two
walk
want (s)
was
water
were
what
where
would
wrote
you
your

Decodable High-frequency Words

after
am
and
as
ask
at
be
best
big
but
can
did
every
fast
first
five
gave
get
had
has
he
help
her
here
him
his
I
if
in
is
it
just
keep
like
little
make
me
much
my
no
not
off
on
put
ran
ride
say
see
she
so
that
them
then
these
this
three
under
up
us
we
when
which
why
will
with
yes

Aa Bb Cc Dd

Ee Ff Gg Hh

Ii Jj Kk Ll

Mm Nn Oo Pp

Qq Rr Ss Tt

Uu Vv Ww Xx

Yy Zz